TOP HITS
FOR EASY PIANO DUET

ARRANGED BY DAVID PEARL

PLAYBACK+
Speed • Pitch • Balance • Loop

To access audio, visit:
www.halleonard.com/mylibrary

Enter Code
6993-4692-1797-7825

ISBN 978-1-5400-7999-2

Visit Hal Leonard Online at
www.halleonard.com

Contact us:
Hal Leonard
7777 West Bluemound Road
Milwaukee, WI 53213
Email: info@halleonard.com

In Europe, contact:
Hal Leonard Europe Limited
42 Wigmore Street
Marylebone, London, W1U 2RN
Email: info@halleonardeurope.com

In Australia, contact:
Hal Leonard Australia Pty. Ltd.
4 Lentara Court
Cheltenham, Victoria, 3192 Australia
Email: info@halleonard.com.au

DESPACITO

SECONDO

Words and Music by LUIS FONSI,
ERIKA ENDER, JUSTIN BIEBER, JASON BOYD,
MARTY JAMES GARTON and RAMÓN AYALA

Moderate Latin beat, in 2

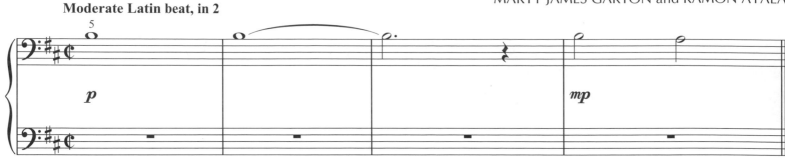

DESPACITO

PRIMO

Words and Music by LUIS FONSI,
ERIKA ENDER, JUSTIN BIEBER, JASON BOYD,
MARTY JAMES GARTON and RAMÓN AYALA

Moderate Latin beat, in 2

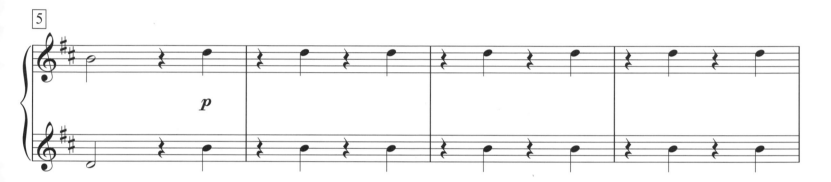

SECONDO

PRIMO

SECONDO

HAVANA

SECONDO

Words and Music by CAMILA CABELLO, LOUIS BELL,
PHARRELL WILLIAMS, ADAM FEENEY, ALI TAMPOSI,
JEFFERY LAMAR WILLIAMS, BRIAN LEE, ANDREW WOTMAN,
BRITTANY HAZZARD and KAAN GUNESBERK

Moderate Latin groove

HAVANA

PRIMO

Words and Music by CAMILA CABELLO, LOUIS BELL,
PHARRELL WILLIAMS, ADAM FEENEY, ALI TAMPOSI,
JEFFERY LAMAR WILLIAMS, BRIAN LEE, ANDREW WOTMAN,
BRITTANY HAZZARD and KAAN GUNESBERK

Moderate Latin groove

SECONDO

Ha - va - na, ooh na   na.

PRIMO

Ha - va - na, ooh na   na.

HIGH HOPES

SECONDO

Words and Music by BRENDON URIE,
SAMUEL HOLLANDER, WILLIAM LOBBAN BEAN,
JONAS JEBERG, JACOB SINCLAIR,
JENNY OWEN YOUNGS, ILSEY JUBER,
LAUREN PRITCHARD and TAYLOR PARX

HIGH HOPES

PRIMO

Words and Music by BRENDON URIE,
SAMUEL HOLLANDER, WILLIAM LOBBAN BEAN,
JONAS JEBERG, JACOB SINCLAIR,
JENNY OWEN YOUNGS, ILSEY JUBER,
LAUREN PRITCHARD and TAYLOR PARX

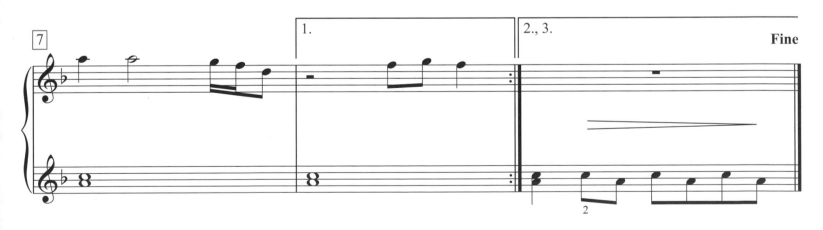

SECONDO

PRIMO

A MILLION DREAMS
from THE GREATEST SHOWMAN

SECONDO

Words and Music by BENJ PASEK
and JUSTIN PAUL

Moderately, with intensity (in 2)

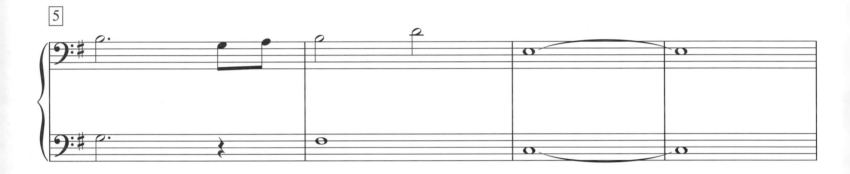

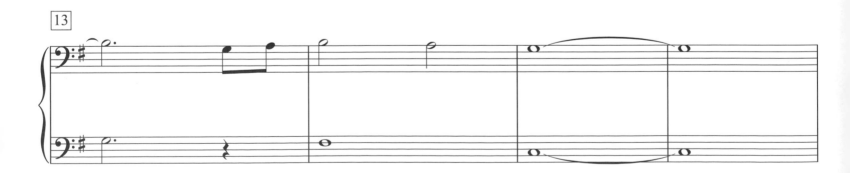

A MILLION DREAMS
from THE GREATEST SHOWMAN

PRIMO

Words and Music by BENJ PASEK
and JUSTIN PAUL

Moderately, with intensity (in 2)

SECONDO

PRIMO

SECONDO

PRIMO

Oh, a mil - lion dreams _ for the world we're gon - na make. _

PERFECT

SECONDO

Words and Music by
ED SHEERAN

Relaxed, in 4

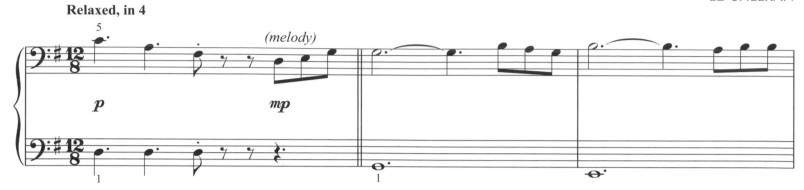

PERFECT

PRIMO

Words and Music by
ED SHEERAN

Relaxed, in 4

SECONDO

PRIMO

SEÑORITA

SECONDO

Words and Music by CAMILA CABELLO,
CHARLOTTE AITCHISON, JACK PATTERSON,
SHAWN MENDES, MAGNUS HØIBERG,
BENJAMIN LEVIN, ALI TAMPOSI
and ANDREW WOTMAN

Moderate Latin groove

I love it when you call me "se-ño-ri-ta"...

SEÑORITA

PRIMO

Words and Music by CAMILA CABELLO,
CHARLOTTE AITCHISON, JACK PATTERSON,
SHAWN MENDES, MAGNUS HØIBERG,
BENJAMIN LEVIN, ALI TAMPOSI
and ANDREW WOTMAN

SECONDO

Ooh, _____ you keep me com - in' for ya.

PRIMO

Ooh, ___ you keep me com - in' for ya.

SHALLOW
from A STAR IS BORN

SECONDO

Words and Music by STEFANI GERMANOTTA,
MARK RONSON, ANDREW WYATT
and ANTHONY ROSSOMANDO

SHALLOW
from A STAR IS BORN

PRIMO

Words and Music by STEFANI GERMANOTTA,
MARK RONSON, ANDREW WYATT
and ANTHONY ROSSOMANDO

SECONDO

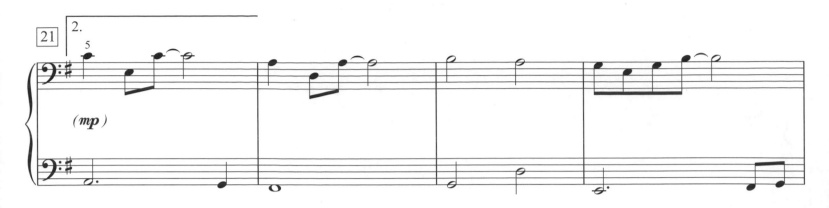

We're far from the shal - low now.

PRIMO

(melody)

We're far from the shal - low now.

SOMEONE YOU LOVED

SECONDO

Words and Music by LEWIS CAPALDI
BENJAMIN KOHN, PETER KELLEHER,
THOMAS BARNES and SAMUEL ROMAN

Moderately

(melody)
mp

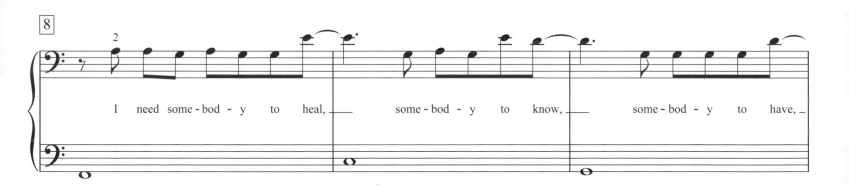

I need some-bod-y to heal, some-bod-y to know, some-bod-y to have,

some-bod-y to hold...

SOMEONE YOU LOVED

PRIMO

Words and Music by LEWIS CAPALDI,
BENJAMIN KOHN, PETER KELLEHER,
THOMAS BARNES and SAMUEL ROMAN

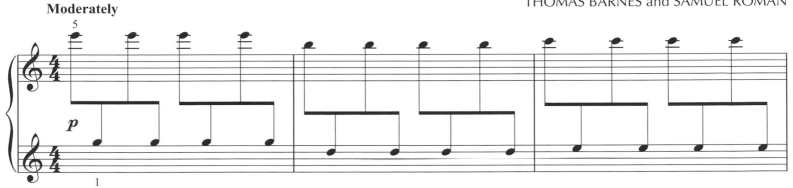

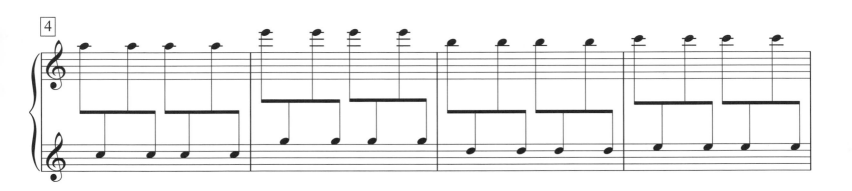

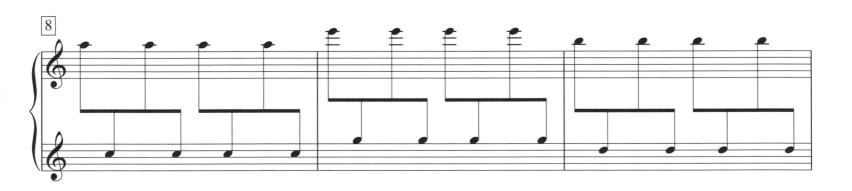

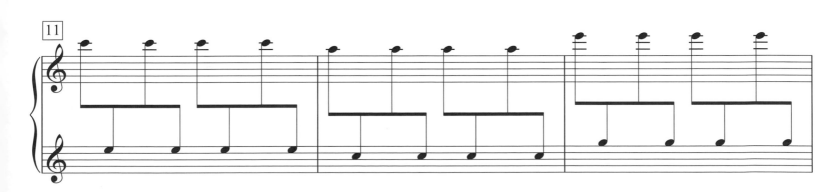

SECONDO

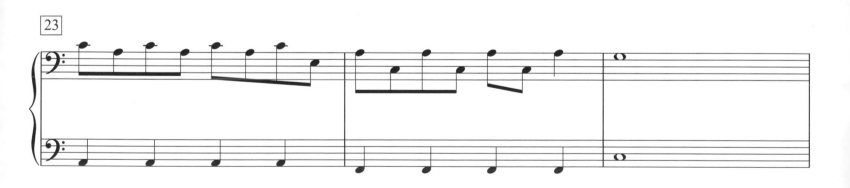

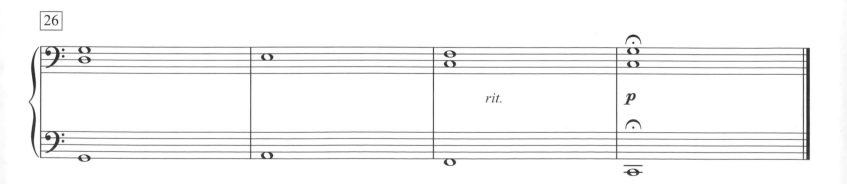

PRIMO

...I was get-ting kind of used to be-ing some-one you loved.

SPEECHLESS
from ALADDIN

SECONDO

Music by ALAN MENKEN
Lyrics by BENJ PASEK
and JUSTIN PAUL

Moderately, in 2

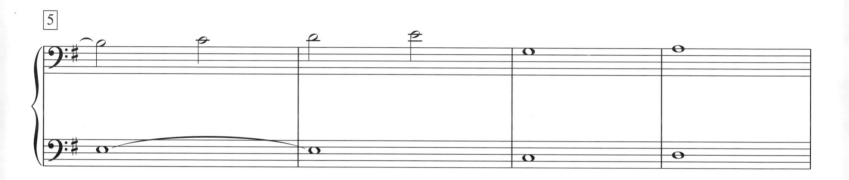

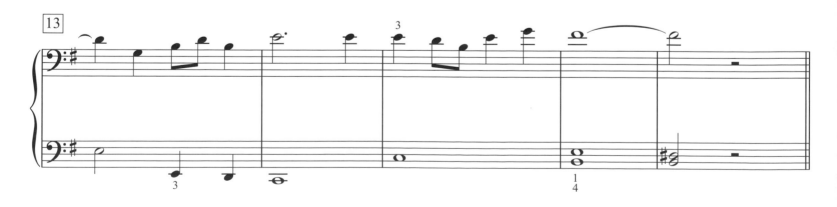

SPEECHLESS

from ALADDIN

PRIMO

Music by ALAN MENKEN
Lyrics by BENJ PASEK
and JUSTIN PAUL

42

SECONDO

PRIMO

SUCKER

SECONDO

Words and Music by NICK JONAS,
JOSEPH JONAS, MILES ALE,
RYAN TEDDER, LOUIS BELL,
ADAM FEENEY, KEVIN JONAS,
HOMER STEINWEISS and MUSTAFA AHMED

SUCKER

PRIMO

Words and Music by NICK JONAS,
JOSEPH JONAS, MILES ALE,
RYAN TEDDER, LOUIS BELL,
ADAM FEENEY, KEVIN JONAS,
HOMER STEINWEISS and MUSTAFA AHMED

We go to- geth- er   bet- ter than birds of a feath- er, you and me...

clap or tap

SECONDO

PRIMO

...I'm a suck-er for you.

PIANO FOR TWO
A Variety of Piano Duets from Hal Leonard

ADELE FOR PIANO DUET
Intermediate Level

Eight of Adele's biggest hits arranged especially for intermediate piano duet! Featuring: Chasing Pavements • Hello • Make You Feel My Love • Rolling in the Deep • Set Fire to the Rain • Skyfall • Someone Like You • When We Were Young.
00172162 1 Piano, 4 Hands.................$14.99

THE BEATLES FOR PIANO DUET
Intermediate Level
arr. Eric Baumgartner

Eight great Beatles' songs arranged for piano duet! Titles: Blackbird • Come Together • In My Life • Lucy in the Sky with Diamonds • Michelle • Ob-la-di, Ob-la-da • While My Guitar Gently Weeps • Yellow Submarine.
00275877 1 Piano, 4 Hands.................$14.99

THE BIG BOOK OF PIANO DUETS

24 great piano duet arrangements! Includes: Beauty and the Beast • Clocks • Edelweiss • Georgia on My Mind • He's a Pirate • Let It Go • Linus and Lucy • Moon River • Yellow Submarine • You are the Sunshine of My Life • and more!
00232851 1 Piano, 4 Hands.................$17.99

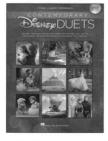

CONTEMPORARY DISNEY DUETS
Intermediate Level

8 great Disney duets: Evermore (from Beauty and the Beast) • How Does a Moment Last Forever (from Beauty and the Beast) • How Far I'll Go (from Moana) • Lava • Let It Go (from Frozen) • Proud Corazon (from Coco) • Remember Me (from Coco) • You're Welcome (from Moana).
00285562 1 Piano, 4 Hands.................$12.99

EASY CLASSICAL DUETS
Book/Online Audio
Willis Music

7 great piano duets to perform at a recital, play-for-fun, or sightread: By the Beautiful Blue Danube (Strauss) • Eine kleine Nachtmusik (Mozart) • Hungarian Rhapsody No. 5 (Liszt) • Morning from Peer Gynt (Grieg) • Rondeau (Mouret) • Sleeping Beauty Waltz (Tchaikovsky) • Surprise Symphony (Haydn). Includes online audio tracks for the primo and secondo part for download or streaming.
00145767 1 Piano, 4 Hands.................$12.99

FAVORITE DISNEY SONGS FOR PIANO DUET
Early Intermediate Level

8 great Disney songs creatively arranged for piano duet: Can You Feel the Love Tonight • Do You Want to Build a Snowman • A Dream Is a Wish Your Heart Makes • Supercalifragilisticexpialidocious • That's How You Know • When Will My Life Begin? • You'll Be in My Heart • You've Got a Friend in Me.
00285563 1 Piano, 4 Hands.................$14.99

FIRST 50 PIANO DUETS YOU SHOULD PLAY

Includes: Autumn Leaves • Bridge over Troubled Water • Chopsticks • Fields of Gold • Hallelujah • Imagine • Lean on Me • Theme from "New York, New York" • Over the Rainbow • Peaceful Easy Feeling • Singin' in the Rain • A Thousand Years • What the World Needs Now Is Love • You Raise Me Up • and more.
00276571 1 Piano, 4 Hands.................$24.99

GOSPEL DUETS
The Phillip Keveren Series

Eight inspiring hymns arranged by Phillip Keveren for one piano, four hands, including: Church in the Wildwood • His Eye Is on the Sparrow • In the Garden • Just a Closer Walk with Thee • The Old Rugged Cross • Shall We Gather at the River? • There Is Power in the Blood • When the Roll Is Called up Yonder.
00295099 1 Piano, 4 Hands.................$12.99

THE GREATEST SHOWMAN
by Benj Pasek & Justin Paul
Intermediate Level

Creative piano duet arrangements for the songs: Come Alive • From Now On • The Greatest Show • A Million Dreams • Never Enough • The Other Side • Rewrite the Stars • This Is Me • Tightrope.
00295078 1 Piano, 4 Hands.................$16.99

BILLY JOEL FOR PIANO DUET
Intermediate Level

8 of the Piano Man's greatest hits – perfect as recital encores, or just for fun! Titles: It's Still Rock and Roll to Me • Just the Way You Are • The Longest Time • My Life • New York State of Mind • Piano Man • She's Always a Woman • Uptown Girl.
00141139 1 Piano, 4 Hands.................$14.99

HEART AND SOUL & OTHER DUET FAVORITES

8 fun duets arranged for two people playing on one piano. Includes: Any Dream Will Do • Chopsticks • Heart and Soul • Music! Music! Music! (Put Another Nickel In) • On Top of Spaghetti • Raiders March • The Rainbow Connection • Y.M.C.A..
00290541 1 Piano, 4 Hands.................$12.99

RHAPSODY IN BLUE
George Gershwin/
arr. Brent Edstrom

Originally written for piano and jazz band, "Rhapsody in Blue" was later orchestrated by Ferde Grofe. This intimate adaptation for piano duet delivers access to advancing pianists and provides an exciting musical collaboration and adventure!
00125150 1 Piano, 4 Hands.................$14.99

RIVER FLOWS IN YOU & OTHER SONGS FOR PIANO DUET
Intermediate Level

10 great songs including the title song and: All of Me (Piano Guys) • Bella's Lullaby • Beyond • Chariots of Fire • Dawn • Forrest Gump - Main Title (Feather Theme) • Primavera • Somewhere in Time • Watermark.
00141055 1 Piano, 4 Hands.................$12.99

TOP HITS FOR EASY PIANO DUET
Book/Online Audio
arr. David Pearl

10 great songs with backing tracks: Despacito (Justin Bieber ft. Luis Fonsi & Daddy Yankee) • Havana (Camila Cabello ft. Young Thug • High Hopes (Panic! At the Disco) • A Million Dreams (*The Greatest Showman*) • Perfect (Ed Sheeran) • Senorita (Camila Cabello & Shawn Mendes) • Shallow (Lady Gaga & Bradley Cooper) • Someone You Loved (Lewis Capaldi) • Speechless (*Aladdin*) • Sucker (Jonas Brothers).
00326133 1 Piano, 4 Hands.................$12.99

www.halleonard.com